Would Rather?

Book For Kids

Mitosha Sulrey Publishing

This Book

BELONGS TO:

○○○○○○○○○○○○○○○○○○○○○○○○○○○○○○○○○

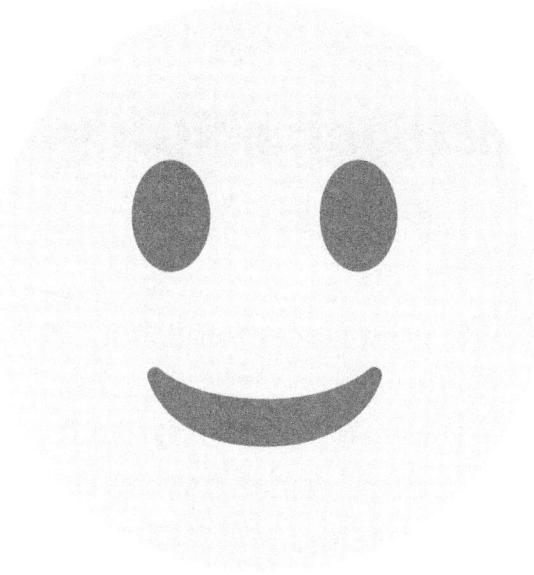

Would You Rather...

be the smartest kid in the class?

OR

the best player in a sports team?

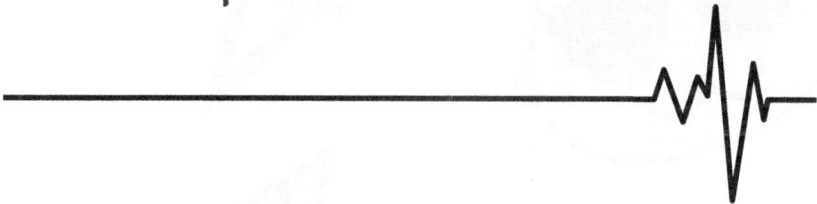

---

eat a giant bug?

OR

get stung by a bee?

Would You Rather...

be the author of a popular book?

OR

a musician in a band who released a popilar album?

---

live in a house shaped like a circle?

OR

a house shaped like a triangle?

Would You Rather...

live in a place with a lot of trees?

OR

live in a place near the ocean?

---

have your room redecorated however you want?

OR

ten toys of your choice (can be any price)?

Would You Rather...

have a magic carpet that flies?

⟲ OR ⟳

a see-through submarine?

---

everything in your house be one color?

⟲ OR ⟳

every single wall and door be a different color?

Would You Rather...

visit the international space station for a week?

OR

stay in an underwater hotel for a week?

have ninja-like skills?

OR

have amazing coding skills in any language?

Would You Rather...

be able to control fire?

OR

water?

---

have a new silly hat appear in your closet every morning?

OR

a new pair of shoes appear in your closet once a week?

Would You Rather...

be able to remember everything you've ever seen or heard?

OR

be able to perfectly imitate any voice you heard?

---

drink every meal as a smoothie?

OR

never be able to eat food that has been cooked?

Would You Rather...

live in a mansion?

 OR

on a farm?

break an arm?

OR

a leg?

Would You Rather...

be able to fly?

(OR)

read minds?

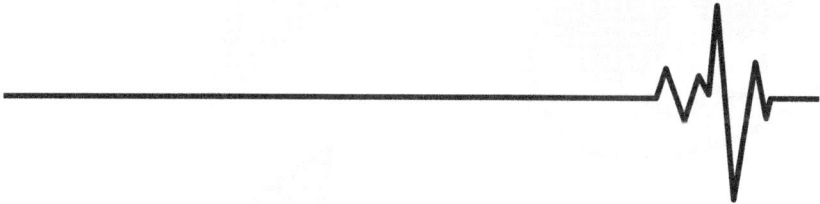

eat chocolate cake?

(OR)

strawberry pie?

Would You Rather...

meet your favorite celebrity?

⟨ OR ⟩

be on a TV show?

be a master at origami?

⟨ OR ⟩

a master of sleight of hand magic?

Would You Rather...

read the book?

⟨ **OR** ⟩

watch the movie?

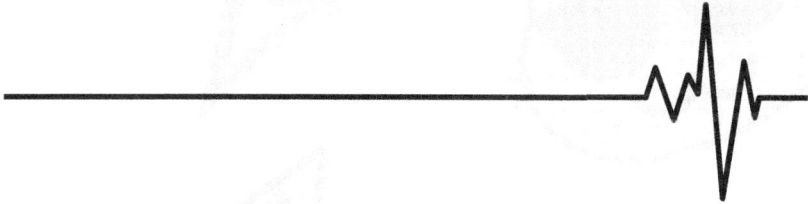

---

be too hot?

⟨ **OR** ⟩

be too cold?

Would You Rather...

have breakfast in hot air balloon?

OR

dinner in a castle?

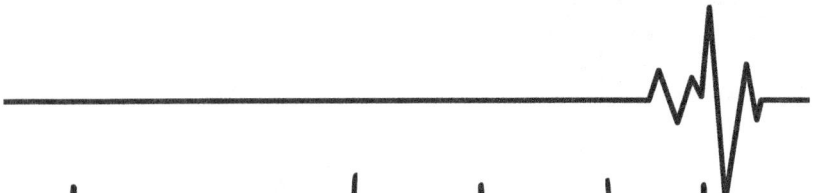

have a dog to skate with?

OR

a pig to ride?

Would You Rather...

have a tail that can't grab things?

OR

wings that can't fly?

_____

dance in front of 1000 people?

OR

sing in front of 1000 people?

Would You Rather...

eat rotten cheese?

 OR

rotten eggs?

---

be the player?

OR

the coach?

Would You Rather...

drink every meal as a smoothie?

OR

never be able to eat food that has been cooked?

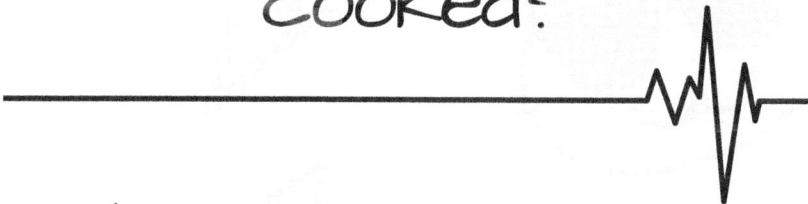

ride a very big horse?

OR

a very small pony?

Would You Rather...

have a missing finger?

OR

an extra toe?

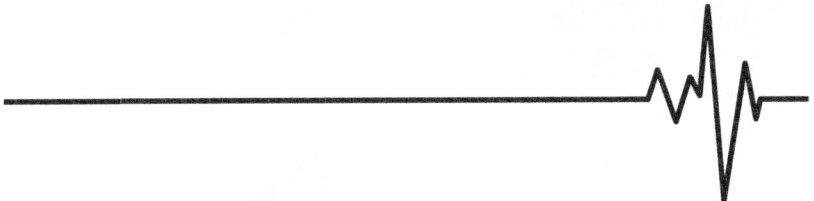

have the ability to fly?

OR

the ability to become invisible?

Would You Rather...

eat a whole stick of butter?

⟅ **OR** ⟆

drink a cup of hot pepper sauce?

---

play at the beach?

⟅ **OR** ⟆

in the snow?

Would You Rather...

be able to move silently?

(OR)

have an incredibly loud and scary voice?

be bulletproof?

(OR)

be able to survive falls from any height?

Would You Rather...

live without music?

〈 **OR** 〉

live without TV and movies?

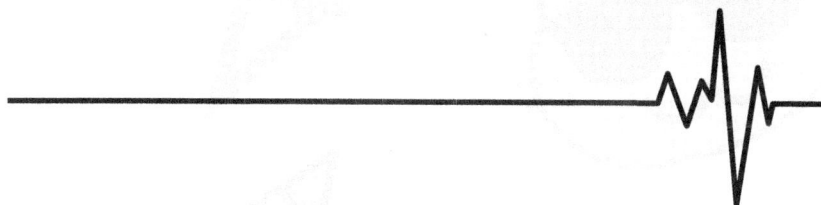

---

meet a famous actor?

〈 **OR** 〉

the President?

Would You Rather...

be incredibly luck with
average intelligence?

OR

incredibly smart with
average luck?

---

be able to change color
to camouflage yourself?

OR

grow fifteen feet taller
and shrink back down
whenever you wanted?

Would You Rather...

live without electricity?

↶ OR ↷

indoor plumbing?

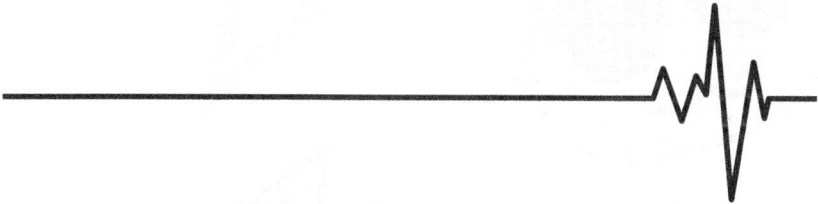

———————————————

be 3 feet tall?

↶ OR ↷

be 8 feet tall?

Would You Rather...

instantly become a grown up?

OR

stay the age you are now for another two years?

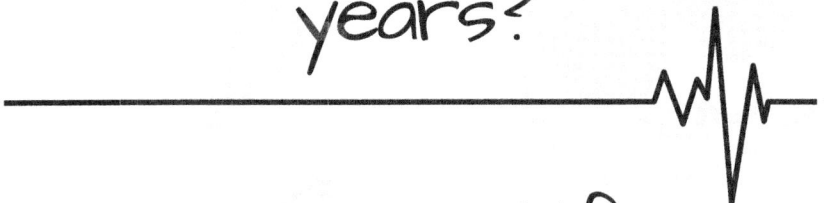

---

have a personal life-sized robot?

OR

a jetpack?

Would You Rather...

run barefoot over
broken glass?

⤸ **OR** ⤴

run barefoot over hot
coals?

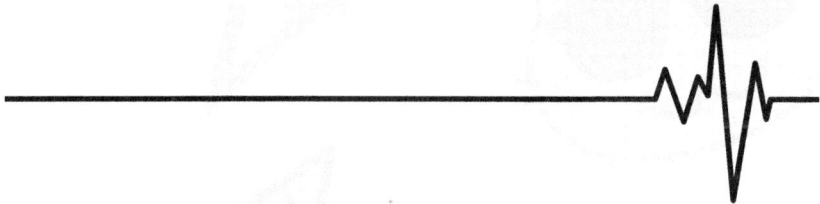

―――――――――

meet an alien?

⤸ **OR** ⤴

a superhero?

Would You Rather...

be a famous singer?

OR

a famous actor?

be a superhero?

OR

a villain?

Would You Rather...

never have any
homework?

⟲ **OR** ⟳

be paid 10$ per hour for
doing your homework?

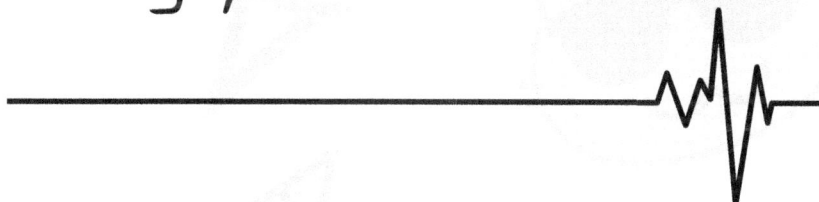

---

take a coding class?

⟲ **OR** ⟳

an art class?

Would You Rather...

have 500 tarantulas crawling in your house?

OR

1000 crickets jumping around your room?

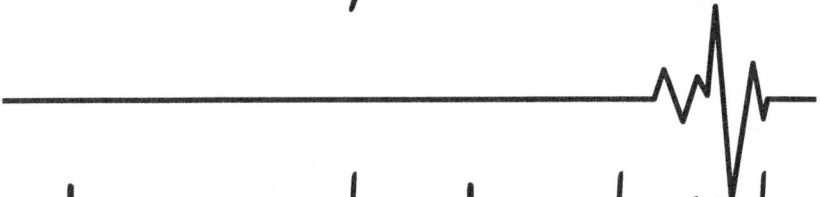

have a dog head and human body?

OR

human head and dog body?

Would You Rather...

live the life of a dog?

§ OR ᒐ

the life of a cat?

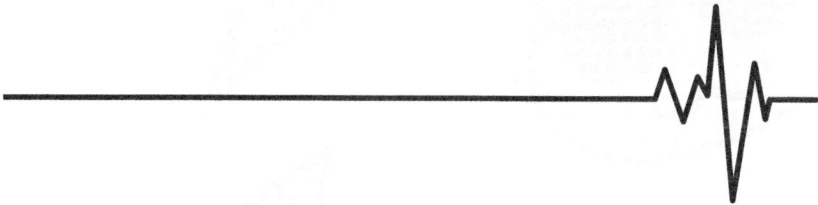

_____

have a unicorn horn?

§ OR ᒐ

a squirrel tail?

Would You Rather...

be able to speak every language in the world?

OR

play every instrument?

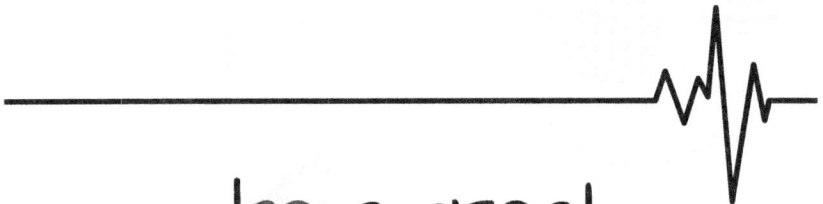

---

be a great skateboarder?

OR

a great juggler?

Would You Rather...

have 10 brothers?

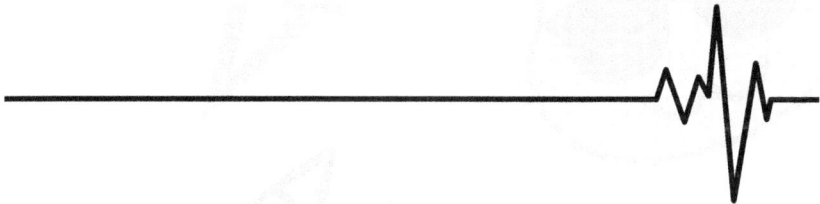 OR

10 sisters?

---

have a robot?

OR

a helper monkey?

Would You Rather...

eat a bowl of spaghetti noodles without sauce?

OR

a bowl of spaghetti sauce without noodles?

---

have eyes that change color depending on your mood?

OR

hair that changes color depending on the temperature?

Would You Rather...

have grass for hair?

⤵ **OR** ⤴

flowers for ears?

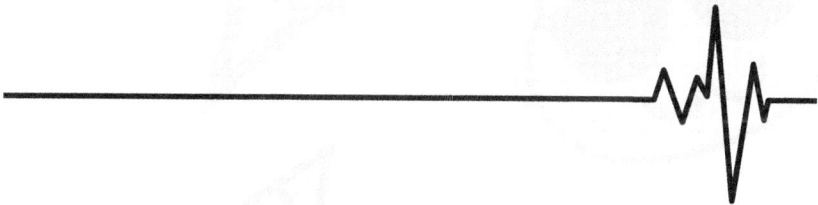

smell like a hamburger?

⤵ **OR** ⤴

smell like a hot-dog?

Would You Rather...

shake hand with an octopus?

(OR)

rub noses with a shark?

_____

have a tiny baby head?

(OR)

tiny baby legs for one year?

Would You Rather...

have hair that smells like chocolate?

OR

smells like vanilla?

---

eat a worm sandwich?

OR

a stinkbug burrito?

Would You Rather...

eat broccoli flavored ice cream?

OR

meat flavored cookies?

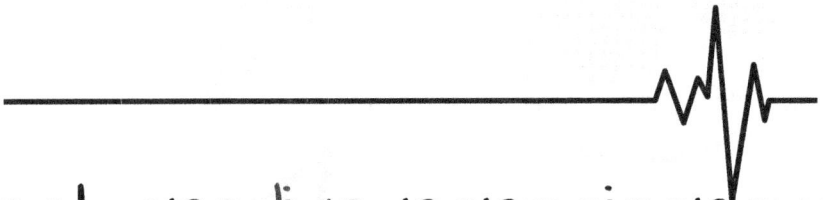

_____

eat one live nonpoisonous spider?

OR

have fifty nonpoisonous spiders crawl on you all at once?

Would You Rather...

have your own
rollercoaster?

↶ OR ↷

your own kid size train

have one huge eye?

↶ OR ↷

three tiny eyes?

Would You Rather...

be the funniest kid in school?

OR

the smartest?

change a stinky diaper?

OR

cleanup barf?

Would You Rather...

live on a sailboat?

⟲ OR ⟳

in a cabin deep in the woods?

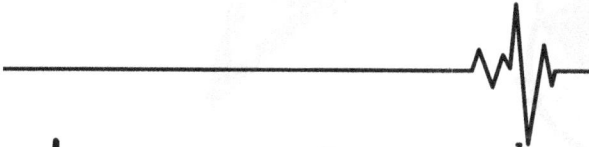

---〜〜---

have an amazing tree house with slides and three rooms?

⟲ OR ⟳

cleanup barf?

Would You Rather...

get shot out of cannon?

(OR)

jump out of a plane?

_____/\/_

be a chicken?

(OR)

a cow?

Would You Rather...

be the best dancer in school?

OR

the best singer?

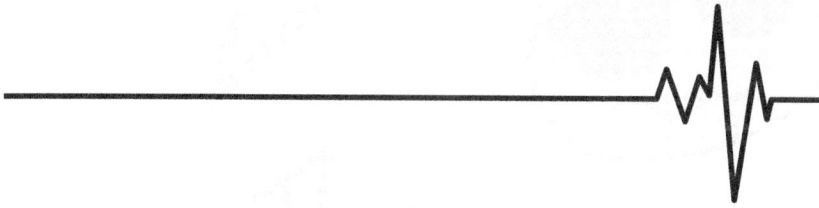

---

never need a shower?

OR

never need to brush your teeth?

Would You Rather...

have a squishy
marshmallow head?

⟳ **OR** ⟳

sticky Popsicle stick leg?

---

sit in the front?

⟳ **OR** ⟳

sit in the back of the
movie theater?

Would You Rather...

wear a super hero cape?

OR

pirate's eye patch for a year?

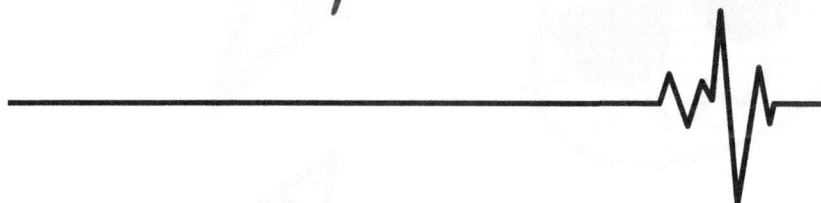

---

have a giraffe neck?

OR

an elephant trunk?

Would You Rather...

have a pig nose?

$ OR ↰

ant eater nose?

---

ride in a submarine?

$ OR ↰

ride on a rocket?

Would You Rather...

sleep in a teepee?

OR

sleep in an igloo?

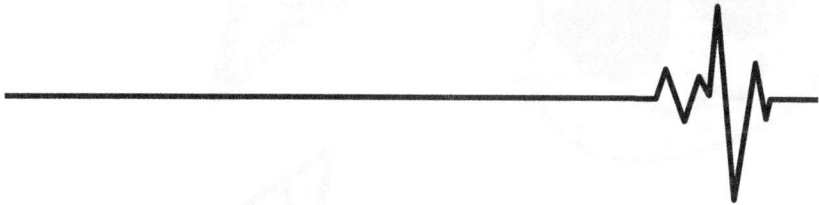

have elephant ears?

OR

a dinosaur tail?

Would You Rather...

be made of metal?

⤹ **OR** ⤸

made of plastic?

have octopus arms?

⤹ **OR** ⤸

caterpillar legs?

Would You Rather...

have your own cruise ship?

⟨ OR ⟩

your own jet airplane?

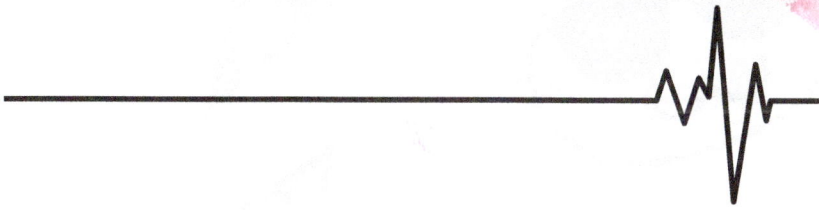

---

have the hiccups all day?

⟨ OR ⟩

sneeze all day?

Would You Rather...

have a new baby brother?

↓ **OR** ↑

new baby sister?

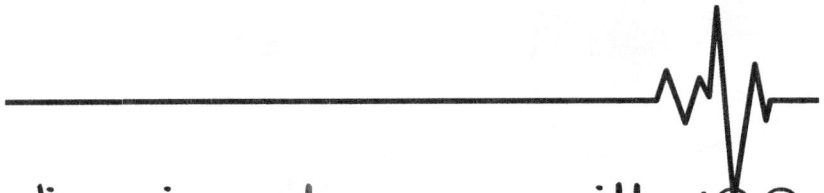

---

live in a house with 100 prickly porcupines?

↓ **OR** ↑

10 stinky skunks?

Would You Rather...

live in a tree?

⟨ **OR** ⟩

live in a cave?

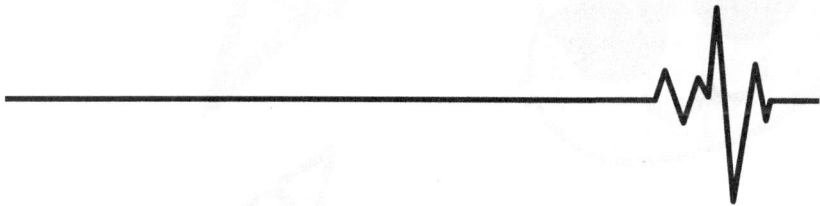

have a time machine?

⟨ **OR** ⟩

a magic wand?

Would You Rather...

ride a piggy?

(OR)

give a piggyback ride?

---

be able to disappear?

(OR)

get really, really big?

Would You Rather...

have bubble gum stuck in
your hair?

OR

step barefoot in doggie
doo?

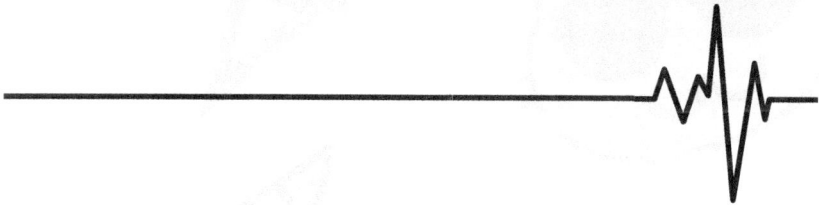

_____

do the dishes?

OR

clean the toilets?

Would You Rather...

eat cookie dough?

(OR)

brownie batter?

fly a kite?

(OR)

fly a drone?

Would You Rather...

take an art class?

 OR

a music class?

---

eat fruits?

OR

vegetables?

Would You Rather...

be a bird?

OR

a fish?

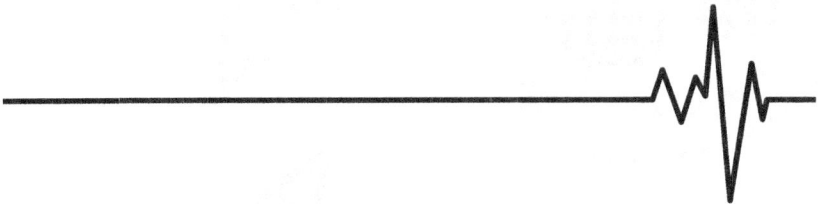

eat spaghetti?

OR

tacos?

Would You Rather...

slide down a rainbow?

↓ **OR** ↑

jump on a cloud?

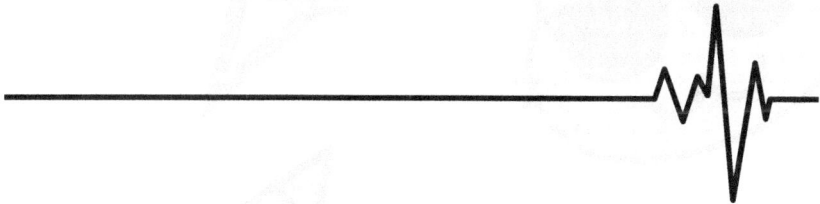

---

grow up fast?

↓ **OR** ↑

stay a kid forever?

Would You Rather...

take bath in ice?

⤸ **OR** ⤴

jello?

---

go to school in your underwear?

⤸ **OR** ⤴

run barefoot in the snow?

Would You Rather...

live at the beach?

⟨ **OR** ⟩

in the mountains?

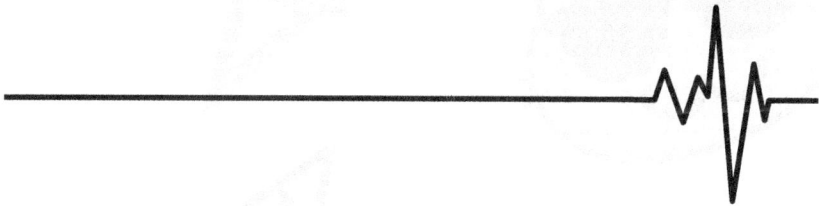

---

have it be winter?

⟨ **OR** ⟩

summer all the time?

Would You Rather...

be able to talk with the animals?

OR

speak any foreign language?

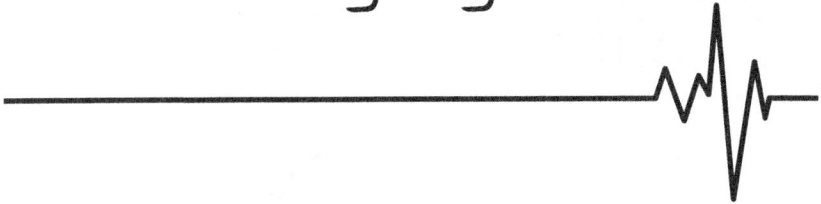

explore space?

OR

the ocean?

Would You Rather...

live on mars?

⤸ OR ⤴

live on the moon?

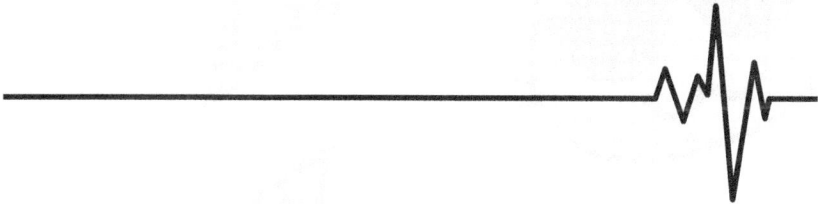

_____

have many good friends?

⤸ OR ⤴

one very best friend?

Would You Rather...

be able to breathe
underwater?

⟨ **OR** ⟩

fly in the air?

―――――――――/\/\―

swim in a pool of jello?

⟨ **OR** ⟩

swim in a pool of
pudding?

Would You Rather...

have a pet dinosaur?

⟨ **OR** ⟩

a robot?

_____

have to swim the entire day?

⟨ **OR** ⟩

stay still the entire day?

Would You Rather...

be an eagle?

OR

a cheetah?

ride on a whale?

OR

an elephant?

Would You Rather...

be the size of an ant?

OR

be the size of a house?

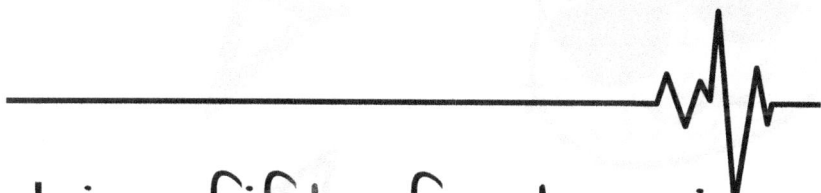

Live fifty feet up in a tree?

OR

live in a cave underground?

Would You Rather...

be older?

 OR

be younger?

---

visit China?

OR

England?

Would You Rather...

be covered in ants?

(OR)

be covered in worms?

---

have cotton balls for hair?

(OR)

corks for teeth?

Would You Rather...

have butterfly wings?

ᘓ **OR** ᘔ

fish fins?

have a pink cat?

ᘓ **OR** ᘔ

a flying horse?

Would You Rather...

loose all your toenails?

OR

loose your eyebrows?

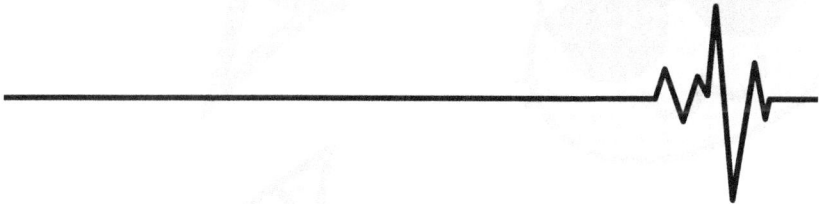

---

be an only child?

OR

have eight siblings?

Would You Rather...

be stepped on by a horse?

⟲ **OR** ⟳

thrown by a gorilla?

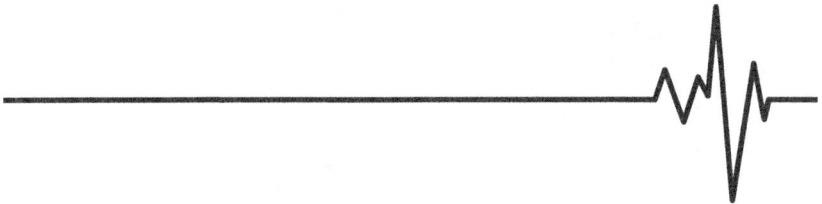

---

have to groom a bear?

⟲ **OR** ⟳

ride a rhino?

Would You Rather...

be incredibly funny?

OR

incredibly smart?

---

have a full suit of armor?

OR

or a horse?

Would You Rather...

be a master at drawing?

⟲ OR ⟳

be an amazing singer?

---

sail a boat?

⟲ OR ⟳

ride in a hang glider?

Would You Rather...

brush your teeth with soap?

⟨ OR ⟩

drink sour milk?

---

be a famous inventor?

⟨ OR ⟩

a famous writer?

Would You Rather...

do school work as a group?

𝄢 **OR** 𝄡

by yourself?

be able to do flips and backflips?

𝄢 **OR** 𝄡

break dance?

Would You Rather...

see a firework display?

⟲ **OR** ⟳

a circus performance?

―――――――――――⋀⋁――――

it be warm and raining?

⟲ **OR** ⟳

cold and snowing today?

Would You Rather...

be able to create a new holiday?

⟨ **OR** ⟩

create a new sport?

---

only be able to walk on all fours?

⟨ **OR** ⟩

only be able to walk sideways like a crab?

Would You Rather...

start a colony on
another planet?

$$OR$$

be the leader of a small
country on Earth?

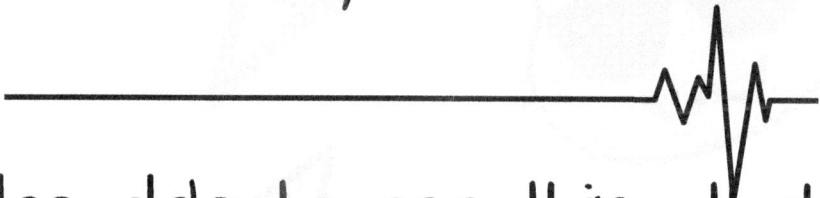

be able to see thing thah
are very far away?

$$OR$$

be able to see things
very close up?

Would You Rather...

be an incredibly fast swimmer?

OR

an incredibly fast runner?

own an old-timey pirate ship and crew?

OR

a private jet with a pilot and infinite fuel?

Would You Rather...

be able to jump as far as a kangaroo?

OR

hold your breath as long as a whale?

---

be able to type/text very fast?

OR

be able to read really quickly?

Would You Rather...

randomly turn into a frog for a day once a month?

OR

radomly turn into a bird for a day once every week?

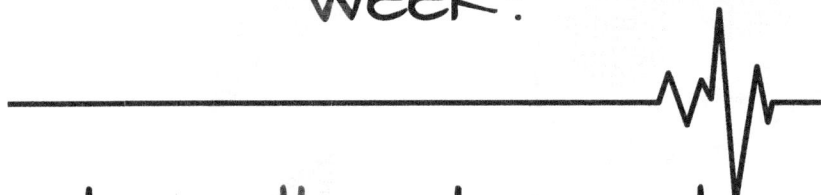

have the chance to design a new toy?

OR

create a new TV show?

Would You Rather...

never eat cheese again?

(OR)

never drink anything
sweet again?

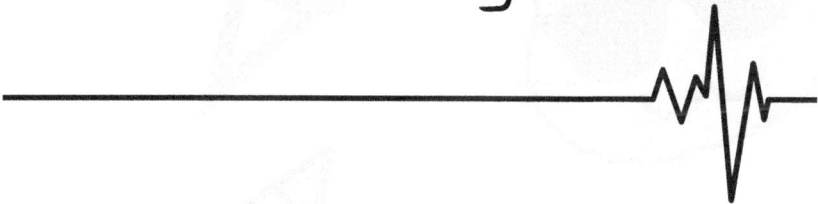

_____

have a cupcake?

(OR)

a piece of cake?

Would You Rather...

be able to move wires around with your mind?

ç OR ʃ

be able to turn any carpeted floor into a six-foot deep pool of water?

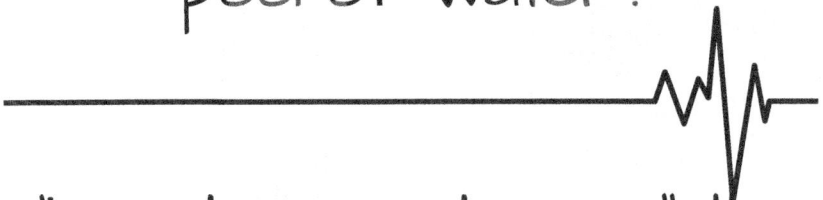

---

live a house where all the walls were made of glass?

ç OR ʃ

live in an underground house?

Would You Rather...

stay a kid until you turn 80?

 OR

instantly turn 40?

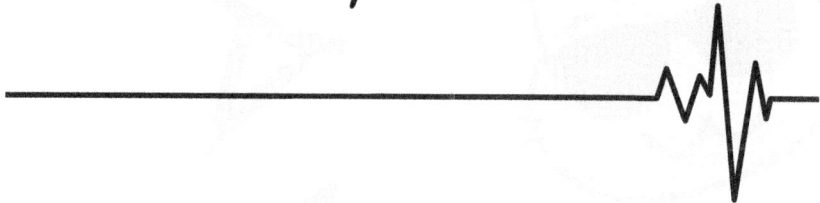

be an athlete in the Summer Olympics?

 OR

the Winter Olympics?

Would You Rather...

be able to watch any movies you want a week before they are released?

OR

always know what will be trendy before it becomes a trend?

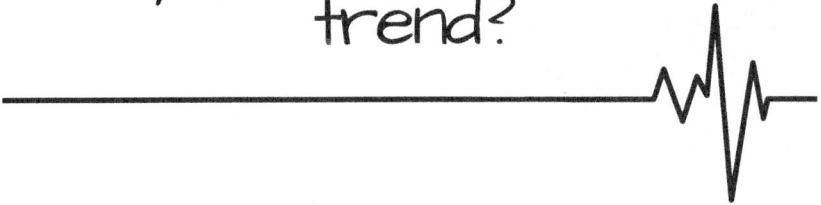

be fluent in 10 languages?

OR

be able to code in 10 different programming languages?

Would You Rather...

be able to find anything that was lost?

OR

every time you touched someone they would be unable to lie?

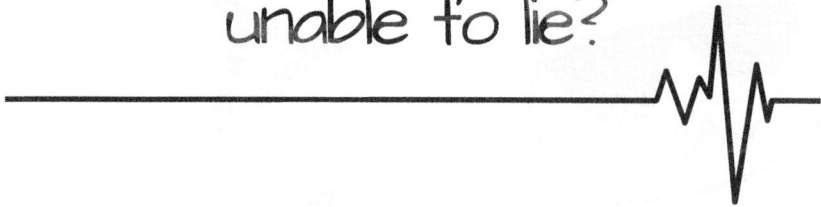

---

open one 5$ present every day?

OR

one big present that costs between 100$ to 300$ once a month?

Would You Rather...

have an unlimited supply of
ice cream?

(OR)

a popular ice cream flavor
named after you?

live in a place that is always
dusty?

(OR)

always humid?

Would You Rather...

have any book you wanted for free?

OR

be able to watch any movie you wanted for free?

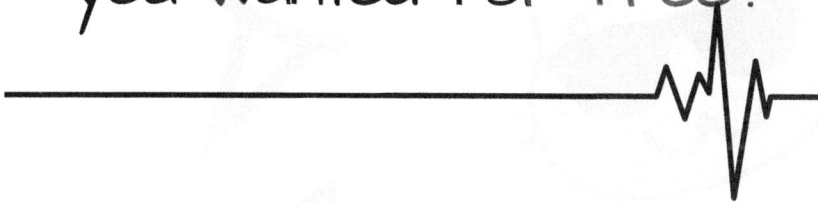

be able to play the piano?

OR

the guitar?

Would You Rather...

be able to read lips?

OR

know sign language?

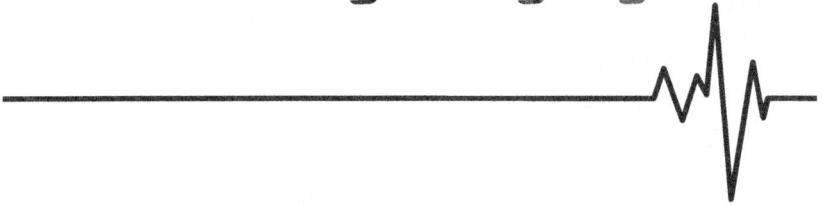

---

have super strong arms?

OR

super strong legs?

Would You Rather...

be able to change the color of anything with just a thought?

OR

know every language that has every been spoken on Earth?

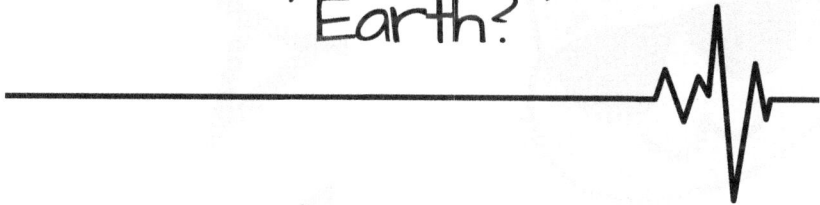

move to a different city?

OR

move to a different country?

Would You Rather...

be wildly popular on the social media platform of your choice?

OR

have an extremely popular podcast?

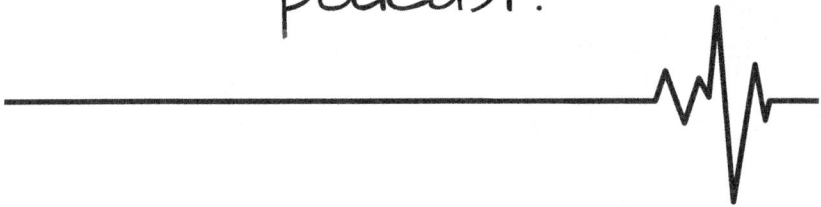

_____

never have to sleep?

OR

never have to eat?

Would You Rather...

be an amazing photographer?

⟲ OR ⟳

amazing writer?

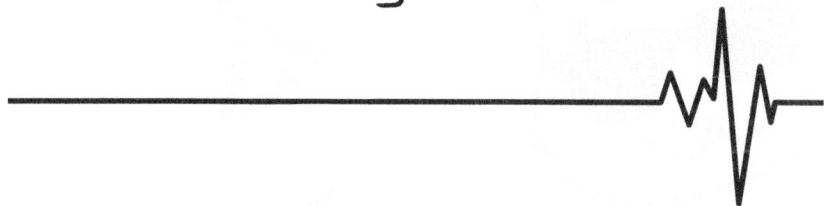

―――――――――――/\/\―――

sneeze uncontrolably for 15 minutes once every day?

⟲ OR ⟳

sneeze once every 3 minutes of the day while you are awake?

Would You Rather...

be able to remember everything in every book you read?

(OR)

remember every conversation you have?

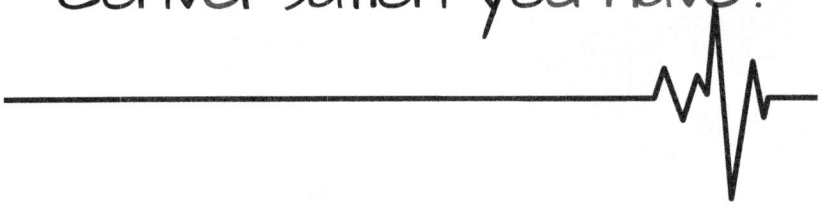

have 10 mosquito bites?

(OR)

one bee sting?

Would You Rather...

be an actor/actress in a movie?

(OR)

write a movie script that would be made into a movie?

ride a roller coaster?

(OR)

go down a giant water slide?

Would You Rather...

get every Lego set that comes out for free?

OR

every new video game system that comes out for free?

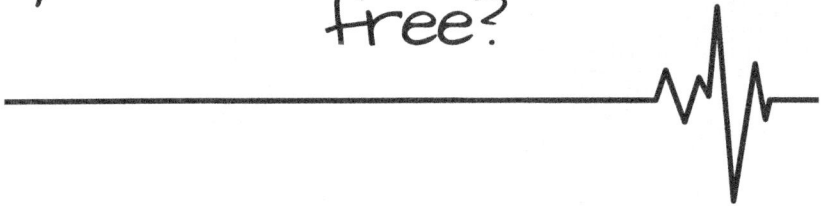

---

go on vacation to a new country every summer?

OR

get an extra three weeks of summer break?

Would You Rather...

eat a turkey sandwich with vanilla ice cream inside?

⟳ OR ⟲

eat vanilla ice cream with bits of turkey inside?

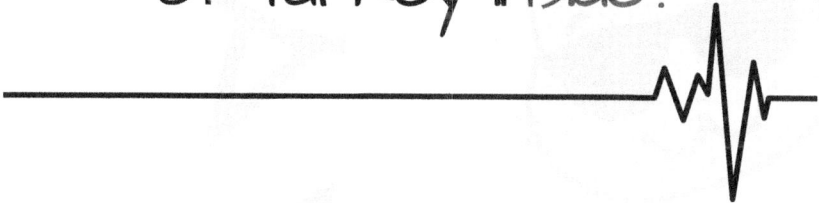

---

visit every country in the World?

⟳ OR ⟲

be able to play any musical instrument?

Would You Rather...

control the outcome of any coin flip?

OR

be unbeatable at rock, paper, scissors?

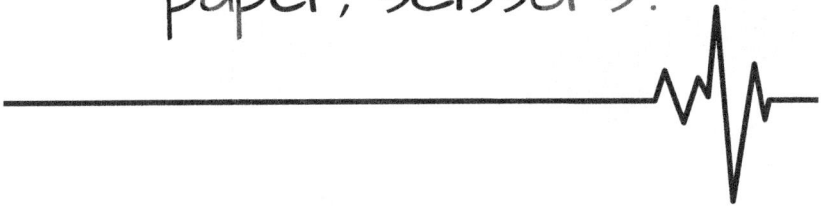

be able to type faster than anyone?

OR

speak faster than anyone?

Would You Rather...

have a private movie
theater?

⟲ **OR** ⟳

your own private arcade?

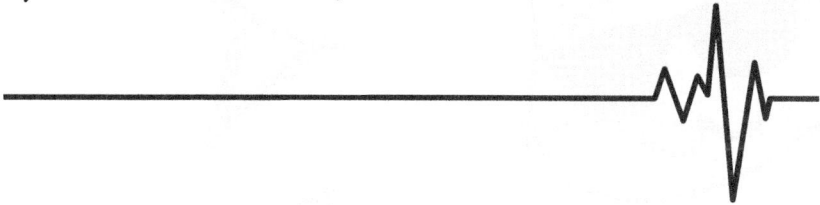

―――――――――――〜⋀⋀〜―――

ride in a hang glider?

⟲ **OR** ⟳

skydive?

Would You Rather...

all water you drink taste like a different delicious beverage every time you drink it?

OR

every vegetable you eat taste like candy but still be healthy?

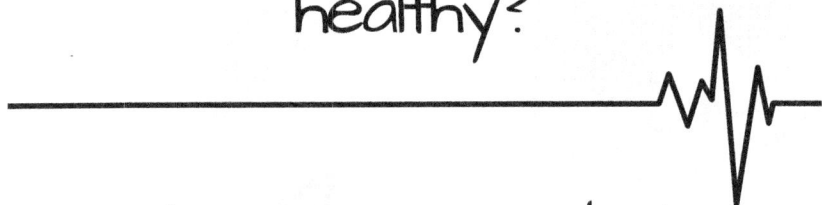

_____

be really good at skateboarding?

OR

really good at any video game you tried?

Would You Rather...

lay in a bathub filled with worms for 5 minutes?

OR

lay in a bathub filled with beetles that don't bite for 5 minutes?

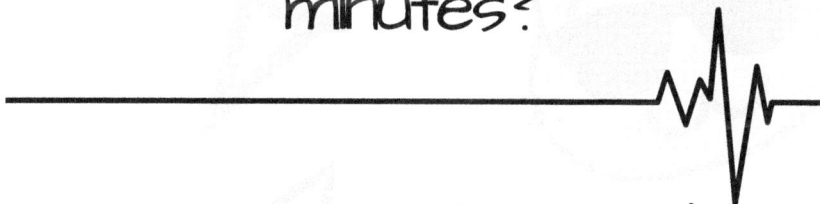

---

have a room with whiteboard walls that you can draw on?

OR

a room where the whole ceiling is one big skylight?

Would You Rather...

have a house with trampoline floors?

↶ **OR** ↷

house with aquarium floors?

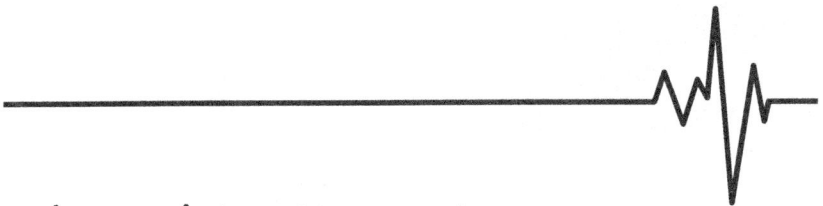

be able to eat any spicy food without a problem?

↶ **OR** ↷

never be bitten by another mosquito?

Would You Rather...

never have to take a bath/shower but still always smell nice?

OR

never have to get another shot but still be healthy

be able to see new colors that no other people could see?

OR

be able to hear things that no other humans can hear?

Would You Rather...

have a very powerful
telescope?

OR

very powerful microscope?

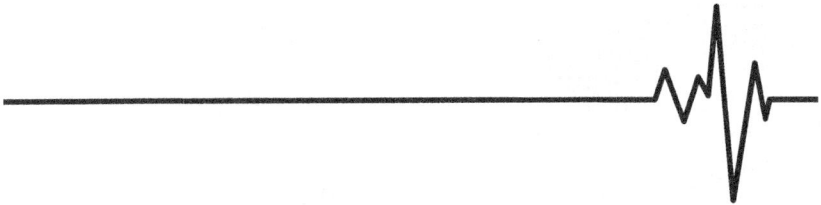

---

be able to change colors like
a chameleon?

OR

hold your breath underwater
for an hour?

Would You Rather...

eat your favorite food every day?

$ OR $

find 5 dollars under your pillow every morning?

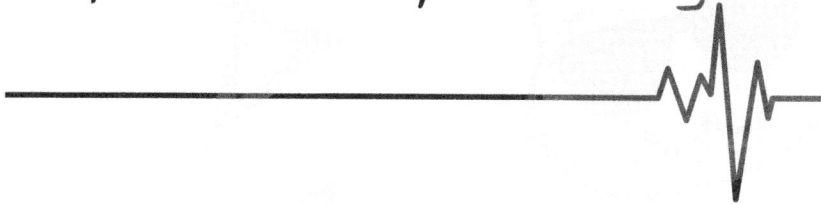

---

have a pet penguin?

$ OR $

a pet Komodo dragon?

Would You Rather...

have a slide that goes from your home's roof to the ground?

OR

be able to change and control what color the lights are in your home?

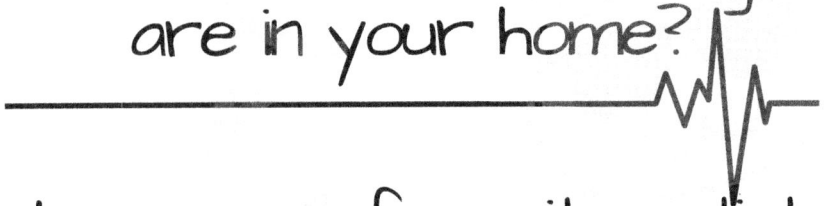

have your favorite artist perform a private show just for you?

OR

perform on stage next to your favorite artist for thousands of people?

Would You Rather...

be the fastest swimmer on earth?

OR

the third fastest runner on earth?

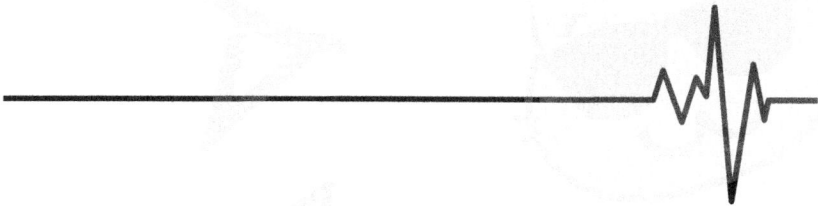

be able to make plants grow very quickly?

OR

be able to make it rain whenever you wanted?

THANK YOU
FOR
PURCHASING

Printed in Great Britain
by Amazon